The
Mystic Mantra
Om Mani Padme Aum

The
Mystic Mantra
Om Mani Padme Aum

Robert Chaney

Foreword by Swami Parampanthi

Astara's Library of Mystical Classics

Published by

Astara

792 West Arrow Highway
Upland, CA 91785

Cover Design
Steve Doolittle

Library of Congress Catalogue Card 99-72963

Printed in the United States of America

Dedicated to the memory of my father,

GALEN CHANEY,

my first and best teacher.

Acknowledgments

Several special people helped bring this book from a simple idea to a tangible reality. The author, and the publisher, are grateful for their help and herewith express their appreciation to:

Sita Chaney, Ph.D., editor
Steve Doolittle, editor, marketing
Beth Hickerson, design, typesetting
Jeffrey Meyer, editor, production coordinator
Swami Parampanthi, writer, teacher, consultant
Pam Rau, editor, manuscript preparation

"OM MANI PADME HUM"

Om, the jewel, is in the lotus Spark
        Of that Divine, primeval Flame
        Whence issuing all spirits came;
Breath of All Life, when understood,
           The Infinite, Eternal Good.

Om, the jewel, is in the lotus Germ,
        Tenebrous, Isis-veiled and hidden,
        Waiting, until from mandate bidden
Cometh the quickening to be
           Sent forth from Life's Infinity.

Om, the jewel, is in the lotus Root
        And stem and tiny, trembling leaf,
        Girded and swathed in watery sheaf
Shadows darkling around, above,
           Murmurous monody of Love.

Om, the jewel, is in the lotus Bud,
        Whispering of untold mysteries,
        Voices of wondrous prophecies,
Gray of mornings, all Divine,
           Bursting to tints Incarnadine!

Om, the jewel, is in the lotus Flower!
        White of the Soul; Gold of the Day,
        Where the iridescent waters play!
O breath of me! O heart of me!
           Life of all life Eternally!

Om, the jewel, is in the lotus Dew!
        Distilled in the Alembic, known
        By Love's pure Alchemy alone;
Sacred Seal and Signet Sign!
           The Life! The Cross of Light Divine!

"OM MANI PADME HUM"
(From the book, "Psychosophy,"
   by Rev. Cora L.V. Richmond)

Contents

Foreword

It is with great pleasure that I write this Foreword to a timely and unique book, *The Mystic Mantra: OM MANI PADME AUM,* by my good friend of many decades and a fellow pilgrim on the path, Dr. Robert Chaney.

Dr. Chaney does not need any introduction to thousands of Astarians, friends and seekers all over the world. He, in conjunction with his life-partner Earlyne Chaney, a supremely gifted mystic, teacher and visionary, has guided and inspired truth-seekers through their books, seminars, lectures, counseling and personal contacts.

To his and our great sorrow Earlyne is no longer on this plane. But their great work continues. Dr. Chaney, ably assisted by their enormously talented daughter Sita and loyal, dedicated and efficient associates, is continuing the worldwide ministry. I am sure that Earlyne's spirit is a guiding force.

A few words about mantra, the subject matter of this book. It consists of a sacred word, words or phrase. It can be in any language. It is an effective tool used daily in spiritual practices in all major religions and even by indigenous people. Its sound, which is considered by certain mystics to be the Mother of all creation, has deep mystical meaning and life-transforming power. Mantra triggers the epiphany of divine power hidden within the consciousness of the chanter. It concentrates the mind for meditation by blocking profane stimuli; it opens the psychic center or Chakras, in some instances filling the chanter with God-consciousness and ineffable peace. It shields the user from destructive or negative forces. It is very popular because it is easy to remember and use at any time or place whenever one needs it the most.

In this book, Dr. Chaney has taken an ancient mantra, sacred to both Hindus and Buddhists, and millions of seekers of truth all over the world, *OM MANI PADME AUM,* and made it, with his superb skill, clearly intelligible to modern men and women of the Western world.

He has explained its significance as an effective mantra; he has outlined the specific methods and exercises that can be used by all seekers to fully utilize this Mantra for prayer, meditation, healing, self-protection, inner growth and spiritual illumination.

He has gone deeper into the mystical implication of the Mantra and explored its various phenomenal and noumenal dimensions which will light the pathway for man's spiritual journey. Both esoteric and exoteric aspects of it have been explained.

Dr. Chaney has interpreted the meaning and various ramifications of the Mantra especially for the Western audience, using terms, ideas and frames of reference familiar and intelligible to them without in any way compromising the essential truth of it. This is, in my opinion, the mark of an excellent teacher. During my forty years of teaching Eastern wisdom in the Western world, I have done exactly the same. What is the benefit of a mantra if it is incomprehensible to people who want to use it?

He has not confined himself to only a traditional interpretation of the Mantra. He has ventured into a novel realm using innovative insights to show the Mantra's many-sided potentiality and uses. This endeavor is extremely beneficial for mantra users.

I want to make a final observation. I am a writer of some skill and have written quite a few books. I have always marveled at Dr. Chaney's ability to explain abstract and difficult concepts in clear, precise and elegant language. He does not use any unnecessary or superfluous words. He is always brief, to the point and crystal-clear in his presentation. He is focused on the essential without straying into peripheral matters. The reader, therefore, will have no trouble in understanding the meaning and various aspects of the Mantra and in following his instructions for its manifold uses. I have read the book with joy and I highly recommend it to all. I wish the book a great success.

Swami Parampanthi
1999
Los Angeles

Preface

OM, spell it OM or AUM, is a word so ancient that its original and literal meaning has been lost in the limbo of time. Its magic, however, has never disappeared. It may be the most powerful word known to humankind.

As a modern word OM possesses literally hundreds of meanings. It is spoken or chanted daily by millions of people around the world. It is uttered more often than any other word in human language.

OM is spoken or chanted by itself or as part of a mystical mantra: OM MANI PADME AUM. What, exactly, is a mantra? It's a word, such as OM, or a phrase, OM MANI PADME AUM, that when thought, spoken or chanted contains and radiates unlimited amounts of energy. It's the spiritual counterpart of a one-a-day vitamin. From the mystic tradition, the single word mantra, OM, is considered to be so filled with energy that many think of it as the vibrational name or symbol of God.

Pronunciation of the words and ways to use the mantra and what it can accomplish in your life will be explored through these pages. I suggest that you read this study with a Zen attitude as opposed to a "high-speed freeway consciousness." The most mystical and ancient of all mantras deserves the deliberate attunement of your consciousness to remote antiquity. Thus you may discover for yourself — or rediscover, many thoughts, ideas, truths, hidden in the ancient wisdom, but containing rays of Light for the perceptive modern mind.

One is apt to repeat the mantra by rote, learning merely the word sounds, unaware of deep implications and great meanings inherent in them. The objective of this study is to offer you a measure of understanding of the words most frequently spoken on this planet, words vibrating in human minds more often than any others. They embrace meanings so numerous it would be impossible to tell all of them. I doubt that any one person even knows them all. Therefore, I have selected those deemed most important, those I feel will activate the greatest power and influence in your life.

To appreciate the mantra and use it effectively requires a recognition of the mystical and esoteric in your life. This is not to say that it has no value in the purely physical level of reality. In truth, it is an excellent vehicle for introducing higher levels of reality into the lower, for merging the vibrational energies and qualities of both levels, resulting in better balance and greater satisfaction in even the most mundane activities.

As I write this, thinking of the physical/spiritual relationship created by using the mantra, I realize there is no physical activity or problem which cannot be helped by it. Nor is there any spiritual longing that cannot be brought closer to attainment by it.

From the ancient Tibetan teachings comes the view that "OM MANI PADME AUM is the heart that has become wise, and the mind that has become spiritual."

Robert Chaney
Upland, California
July, 1999

The
Mystic
Mantra

The Mystic Mantra:
OM MANI PADME AUM

History tells us that in olden times the one nation that paid but little heed to materiality and devoted itself almost exclusively to spirituality was India. How could that occur?

It is the general supposition that in prehistoric times a few groups and many individuals in India and Tibet for centuries lived in isolation from the rest of the world. During that time they were free from commerce and conquest, their minds undisturbed by strategies of buying and selling, the manufacture of instruments of war, or the desire to conquer and enslave other lands and people. Unless we are driven by the unreasonable doctrine of exclusivity — stated as "my religion is the only true religion" — we should be thankful for this historical saga of spirituality.

The spiritual concepts developed so long ago ultimately found their way into most modern spiritual philosophies. An examination of the scriptures of many religions contain the thoughts found in Hindu scriptures of a far earlier time. Many of our words, spiritual or not, flowed from the fountains of Sanskrit, as your dictionary will depict on page after page. OM MANI PADME AUM may be the most important of all.

To begin our journey back through the ages in search of hidden and mystic interpretations of the mantra, OM MANI PADME AUM, we find it said among many people of Oriental lands that in the beginning the Supreme One came into existence upon a lotus petal. Lest you think that thought minimizes the original One, consider its symbology for a moment.

Judeo-Christian biblical symbology describes a portion of creation with the words "In the beginning God created the heaven and the earth. And the earth was without form, and void; and darkness was upon the face of the deep." Then it states that the spirit of God, or the breath of God, moved upon the face of the waters and created light.

Compare the Biblical version with the pre-Christian idea of a Great Being of Light, practically weightless, suddenly appearing upon a lotus petal supported on the surface of earthly waters. Same story. Different version. Different symbology. In both versions the Divine Being amassed the forces of creativity at a "moment," perhaps millenniums in length in earth planet history — and from then on the creation process proceeded with comparative swiftness.

After this symbolic appearance on the waters of life, the Oriental version continues with the Supreme One creating the word OM. That word, with all its vibratory connotations, was used to create all that exists. Its vibrational energy became the seed of all human thought and knowledge. The Gospel of John states, "In the beginning was the Word, and the Word was with God, and the Word was God." Thus both Hindu and Christian philosophy use sound, the vibrational quality of a word, or thought, to tell the creation story.

The ancients passed to their devotees the idea that OM contains energies beyond the limitations and definitions of everyday words. It is a word to be spoken or chanted, of course, but beyond that it is a word to be *experienced.* The use of OM can lead to the ultimate experience of feeling that the inner individualized infinite and its connection with the greater Universal Infinite is truly known beyond words.

It is said by some that the sound of O, first letter of OM, stirred the vibrational energies which brought the heavens, the earth and the waters of the seas into existence. It is spoken by the sustained sounding of "oh" with lips slightly opened.

The second letter or sound is spoken without interruption simply by closing the lips, producing an "mmm" sound. It is with this vibratory combination of "oh" and "mmm" that sun, moon and stars were said to have been created.

The two sounds are spoken or chanted as one word, similar to the word "home" without the "h" sound.

OM is considered the most powerful word of the full mantra. It is often used alone to reinforce the energy of a creative thought or act. To experience a hint of its power, simply close your eyes, chant the word, verbally holding the "oh" and "mmm" sounds for an equal length of time. Note how the sound reverberates throughout your chest and head areas, specially in the third eye centers (throat, pituitary and pineal glands), as well as the heart.

We shall examine the mystic mantra in several ways; word by word, syllable by syllable and as a complete phrase. To attempt literal translation of the mantra or any of its individual parts would be difficult even for a scholar of Sanskrit. In the same way it is difficult to understand most all spiritual scriptures in their literal sense.

OM is a word of numerous meanings and at this point we shall consider but a few of them. More will be examined in later pages.

"Hail" is one of the meanings. It isn't a casual "hello." It is the voice of recognition and acceptance between lower and higher aspects of your own being, between your self and your Self. Or between you and still higher dimensions, even an attribute of the Supreme One. It is a way of saying, "Hello God. Here I am, getting in touch with You."

"Hail," sounded through the word OM, implies you are vocalizing a personal and harmonious coherence with the Divine. It alludes to your keeping that spiritual fusion inviolate and purified within yourself. You are recognizing and maintaining a sacred meeting place in the holy of holies within your own being.

OM also expresses an amen. Or "so be it." As such it is not merely a word of closure, as the end of a prayer. It signifies the outpouring of an inner energy into whatever is to follow. OM and amen do share a similar sound, create a similar vibration and are used for similar purposes. More on the word OM later.

MANI means "an ever-shining jewel." Not an ordinary gem by any means, but one that is the repository of an eternally radiating light. It is this jewel, hidden within the leaves or sheaths of your being, that radiates your inner light into the outer world around you. The jewel often considered in this connection is the diamond. Because of its many faceted nature it represents incorruptibility, purity and invincibility.

MANI may also represent "the Blue Light of the void" mentioned in the Tibetan Book of the Dead. Here the *blue* signifies not the color blue, but the clarity of the radiance, like the 'blue sky.'

MANI also means "thunderbolt." In this sense it represents the highest of vibrational energies that occasionally burst upon the physical plane with the overwhelming power of sound and light combined.

PADME refers simply to the lotus, rooted in the mud of the earth, opened to the light of the sun, quickened by the transcendental presence of the Supreme One.

The spiritual lotus is purified by the life processes that occur within it, and through it. It is more than a mere flower of enticing scent and beauty. It is the divine flowering *principle*, ever opening, ever unfolding, ever blossoming in all humankind and in each individual.

AUM is similar in meaning to OM, AND is sometimes spelled HUM. It also indicates a "so-be-it" or an amen. The difference is that OM is a statement of beginning, bringing into existence: AUM or HUM is a declaration of completion. Through it, the spiritual forces of creation have been transported into the realm of physical substance. The physical has been blessed by the presence of the spiritual. The energy of fruition brings completion to the energy of creation.

Another view of the relation between OM and AUM as used in the mantra is that the energies of OM are those used in opening the self to the vibrational presence of the divine — while the energies of AUM are those used in projecting the divine presence through the self into the surrounding world. Thus the divine is flowing constantly in and out of the human individual who speaks the mantra.

It is also related to the Sanskrit word "*showhum*," I am He, or I am God. This word is also used as a mantra by Hindus to assist the chanter in finding his/her oneness with God.

OM MANI PADME AUM. Let us now examine the mystic mantra as a unified statement rather than as a series of separate words.

In the long ago, these words were never committed to written form, for it was considered sacrilegious — the creation of an idol — to do so. Placing an "eternal idea," which partook of divinity, on a temporal object that would succumb to the ravages of time and humankind, was considered an extreme act of disrespect. It is understandable that the ancients wished to preserve the purity of thoughts or energies proceeding from Divine Mind to human mind by not consigning them to objects subject to certain disintegration. Thus the words and their meanings were regarded as an inner treasure to be conveyed only to the select few who would understand and preserve them in consciousness.

There were comparatively few people in the world in those early days. There were no methods of mass production and transmittal as with all communication and preservation media existing today. Distribution via printed, recorded, electronic methods is now possible to billions rather than hundreds. And that is all to the good. The method of transmitting the message is far less important than the message itself. The impact of frequency is essential to keeping the message alive in the twenty-first century.

Listen carefully to yourself as you speak aloud the ancient words OM MANI PADME AUM. Let the words reverberate throughout your being. In any modern language you may actually be saying, "So be it — O Jeweled Lotus — Amen." Which version, the ancient or the modern English, most appeals to you? Both are expressing the same idea. And in either version the sound of your voice (or the physical energy) combined with the expression of your emotional, mental and spiritual energies, kindles the most dynamic spiritual power you are capable of expressing. Conversely, it may soothe, pacify or restore harmony. It depends upon your intent as the words are spoken, either mentally or aloud.

Speak the words with this thought predominately in your mind: "I am the Jewel in the Lotus." I suggest that as you do so you will soon begin to notice a heightened awareness of your spiritual nature. We often accept our spiritual nature on an intellectual level only. The preceding version of the mystic mantra tends to focus your awareness upon your spiritual self with an acute emphasis that may be startling.

As you speak the mantra with these words in mind, "Hail — Jewel in the Lotus — So be it," you may note the ease with which you experience a sense of inner divinity. The ever-shining jewel, or the great thunderbolt of power, are inner images that may accompany this version as you repeat it slowly for several moments. During the process you may also experience receiving, then releasing, a flow of an energy greater than your own. Mystic mantra indeed.

Another approach to speaking the mantra is to direct it mentally toward one or more of the following meanings:

I am unfolding the Jeweled Lotus.
> I bring into expression, from within myself, the
> glory and the power of the Supreme One.

I am unfolding in the avenue of life I have chosen to follow.
> I am unfolding openness and acceptance in my
> relationships.

I am unfolding my spiritual consciousness.

I am unfolding my intuitive senses.

I am unfolding the divinity within me.

I am unfolding my spiritual nature.

> I seek the jewel or Brahman hidden in the Lotus.

I seek the wisdom (Jewel) hidden in the Lotus.

I suggest that you select not more than two of the above meditation ideas to focus on during any one meditation session. In addition to the above, you may wish to phrase your own points of focus for the lotus meditation. Avoid complex statements. Any phrase selected should be one pointed and brief. Always link your lotus statement with the inner feeling of an open receptive sense similar to the manner in which the lotus flower opens to receive the rays of the sun.

You also may wish to experiment with the various meanings and intentions until you discover which one or two most appeal to you. You will notice a greater affinity for some than for others. Continue to use those for which you find a stronger inner attraction until you feel a change is indicated.

Devotion
and
Dedication
— Public
and
Private

Devotion and Dedication —
Public and Private

Around the world, certain Eastern disciplines believe the number, potency and efficacy of their prayers are heightened through the use of prayer wheels. A prayer wheel is simply a circular container holding prayers written on small slips of paper. The idea is that every written prayer is spoken and repeated with each revolution of the container, which may be as small as an ordinary grocery can or as large as a thirty gallon barrel. In China, I have seen, and dropped a written prayer into, more than one of the larger size, probably containing scores of prayer slips. Is the practice merely a religious superstition? I can only say that my prayer was answered.

Some of the prayer wheels, as they are called, contain hundreds of prayer slips on which the only written words are OM MANI PADME AUM, as well as prayers related to specific needs or desires of the petitioners. Monks at the temples turn the containers regularly. In effect, then, OM MANI PADME AUM is "spoken" more often than any other spiritual phrase. And this would be true even without considering the prayer wheels.

At least the whirling wheels illustrate, or symbolize, the tremendous energy that may be activated through using the mantra. The one who speaks OM while inwardly feeling its spiritual significance understands that it represents the essence and elements of the entire universe. It means "All" in such a complete sense as to be inconceivable by the human mind. In other words, it is beyond intellectual thought and into the higher realm of spiritual feeling — an awesome ecstasy of "being one with" a truly universal being. It encompasses all that is, everywhere in space or time.

Experiencing this is not an everyday event. Once in a lifetime will do. The grandeur of it is beyond comprehension.

Not all religions portray the Divine One in the same sense. There are three progressive stages of philosophic thought through which certain religions — and sometimes individuals on their own — will pass in understanding their relationship with the Supreme Being. OM, or OM MANI PADME AUM, is an aid to this understanding.

In one instance, God is a completely separate, manipulative Being, usually masculine in gender. He can be spatially close to the human person or far away. On a mountain top or in a temple. But always a completely separate Entity.

In the second philosophic stage, God becomes selectively incarnate. He expresses a preference for a single person out of the multitudes in whom to incarnate, thus becoming His own son, and in that form delivers messages to those who then deify the messenger. There is nothing particularly wrong with this process except the messenger usually, and sensibly, rejects the deification and points to the third stage, which the Hindus philosophically accepted thousands of years ago.

God — universally incarnate — in you and me and every living thing. When the Hindu writes a note to you the salutation is "Dear Self," the Divine in me greets the Divine in you. God in all persons. When a follower of Hinduism meets you, whether you are friend or stranger, with head bowed and hands prayerfully pressed together, the greeting you will hear is, "Namaste," meaning the Deity in me recognizes and honors the Deity in you.

Theoretically, the God within is not difficult to accept. Experientially, it is another matter. Actually to feel the Presence of the Something Greater than yourself is more than an intellectual exercise. OM will help you do so. Chant it for a few moments now. Open the lotus of your heart, just as a lotus opens to a ray of sunshine. OM...feel the comforting Presence...OM... its warmth...OM...its Light...OM...its Love.

No other single word in human language contains the vibrational lustre found in the word OM.

How
OM Saved
the World

How OM Saved the World

Ages ago, says a legend about the way the word OM saved the world, there arose a gigantic struggle for power between lower beings and the gods. Through evil intent and deceit, the forces of darkness managed to subjugate the lower beings and influence them for the legendary evil purposes of darkness. These evil ones obtained information which increased their power and made them nearly equal with the gods themselves. A tragedy of universal magnitude was imminent. The gods were about to become slaves to the dark forces.

In frantic desperation the gods appealed to the highest force of light, the Supreme One. They were told they must first reclaim control of themselves through calm meditation, thus purifying their own minds. Then they must use the sound of OM to generate its mighty power and direct it to dissolve the lower vibratory forces of darkness. The gods followed directions and gradually regained the supremacy which they had temporarily lost. In fact the word OM was used so successfully that it was given its own reward. It was decreed that no spiritual scriptures were to be spoken, or holy ritual conducted, without including it. In time, it was included in the written as well as the spoken spiritual word, and this may account for using the word AMEN at the close of our prayers today. In many cultures it is the word Om.

This story represents the concept that truth, purity and divinity (or spirituality) combined contain a spiritual vibratory power that is reflected in the single word Om.

OM
Day by Day

Om...Day by Day

When the sun is rising, the mass consciousness of humankind is stirred into convolutions of chaotic activities that clash with uncontrolled fury. Subways and freeways are symbols of the hectic energies released in the process. They sing a song of chaos. Workplaces and homes, families and individuals, need a spiritual oil to calm the troubled waters of life.

Relief comes from the ancient traditions in their many forms. It should be no surprise that among them is the word Om, spoken or chanted, mentally or orally. Perhaps you may want to try it to help calm your troubled waters.

At the beginning of the day, before you are caught up in the frenzy to come, spend a few moments, quietly, peacefully, with Om, the song celestial, the personal melody with special tones that in one way or another introduce harmony into your life...

• as a daily phrase of devotion to the Supreme One. In cultures where Om is a word of reverence, sunrise is greeted with a few quiet moments. As one inbreathes the energies of the new day with every breath inhaled, Om is softly spoken with every exhalation.

• as atonement for an offense. A trespass or negative behavior of any nature requires atonement. It is not implied that

speaking or chanting Om suffices to negate karma or relieve
one of guilt. It does seek the input of a specific spiritual focus
into one's life, and the resulting spiritual energies, that enable
one to acknowledge a karmic responsibility, and help open spiritual channels which aid in making proper recompense.

In certain disciplines, priests assign to one who errs the
task of repeating statements or prayers as penance for a committed sin. Penance and atonement are not the same. A penance, though ascribed by a religious personage, is basically an
act of self-punishment. Punishment does not really pay a debt.
If in some way I cheat you of a thousand dollars and am jailed
for ten days, I have been punished but I have not paid my debt
to you. I have not atoned for it.

Atonement is a spiritual act which is an essential part of
the process of paying a karmic debt. Penance is sacramental
punishment. Atonement is payment. The proper concentration
of spiritual energies changes the consciousness of one who has
misbehaved, changing his pathway from evil to good. It is the
process described by the words "go (or change) and sin no
more."

• as one of many means of self-purification. Centering your
attention on the word Om, or upon the full mantra, Om Mani
Padme Aum, generates a reciprocal reverberation effect.

Strike the C note, or play a C chord, on a piano and all the
C strings, or the C chord strings of the entire piano keyboard
will respond with similar (although less audible) vibrations.
The verbal Om accomplishes something of a similar nature. It

causes responsive vibrational effects in every muscle, gland, organ, bone, and throughout the nerve systems and bloodstream of your body.

Harmonious correspondences also result from your selection of body areas on which to center your attention as you speak or chant your Om. As an experiment, intone or sound a few Oms while keeping your awareness centered in the head or third eye area, including throat, pituitary and pineal chakras, or energy centers. Then sound several with your focus upon your heart chakra, noting the different response feeling as compared to the first step in the experiment. And finally intone more Oms with your solar plexus chakra as the focal point of your awareness. And again note the difference in response feeling.

From this experiment you are quite apt to note three different types of feeling sensations. Continued experiments will enable you to determine which of the three provides you with the most attractive methods of using the mantra. Whichever of the three centers you select matters much less than the thought (idea) in your mind at the time. In general, attention in the solar plexus area relates to physical and etheric body matters. Attention in the heart area pertains also to physical feelings and, in addition, to your emotional nature. And attention to the throat, pituitary and pineal area relates to matters of intuition, mind and spirit.

Remember that with each of the three general areas the process is one of cleansing and purification. A suggestion on this topic that may prove helpful to you is that you are not merely centering your attention on the three areas, you are sounding or speaking *through* them. They are, in turn, replicating your vocal sound *and* your physical, emotional, mental and spiritual intent. A powerful combination.

• for overcoming defects in ritual. In many cultures, both priests and lay persons recite the Oм at the closing of a ritual. They realize that it is impossible to perform an entire ritual perfectly, for perfection is only of God. The mantra is used to signify that any imperfection did not result from human intent. It also signifies that the great energy and love of God are requested so that any defect in the ritual will be erased.

Oм also refers to the assent, "Yes." It is not merely the human yes. It is the affirmative agreement that the human and the divine are one in purpose.

• as a simple moment of attunement with the greater life and its purposes in your life. Dedicate five minutes to speaking or chanting Oм, or the full mantra, with the following intent, or your variation of it:

"Oм...I am one with the Divine One. Oм...may my emotions remain calm, my mind alert, and my spirit coupled with Divine Spirit. Oм...may all my faculties be illumined. Oм...may understanding fill my heart. Oм..."

The
Six Senses
of OM

(You may wish to photocopy this or draw your own version of the Om symbol for convenience in practicing this exercise.)

The Six Senses of OM

In your personal, private relationship with OM as more than a word or spiritual mantra, consider it a resource for experiencing vital life in all your senses. Hearing, seeing, feeling, smelling, tasting and intuitional senses all may be stirred to new heights by this exercise.

As you concentrate on the Sanskrit symbol, and chant the word aloud several times first, listen to its musical tones as one of the most beautiful sounds you will ever hear.

Then, in silence, concentrate visually on the symbol. In time it will glow inwardly with a soft luminescence.

Next, center your attention on the inner feeling you sense throughout your entire body as your thoughts are still on the sound and sight of the symbol.

Then, as you breathe gently and continue to turn inward, you may become aware of an aromatic response, perhaps the aroma of the lotus or another favorite flower. Hold and enjoy it a few moments.

Then, turn your attention to tongue and tastebuds. What flavor does OM give you? Savor it another few moments.

Finally, remain calm, peaceful, relaxed, for the entry of intuitive impulses into your receptive consciousness. Or perhaps you simply will be infused with a sense of spirituality.

Use the Mantra for Self Growth and Achievement

Use the Mantra for Self Growth and Achievement

There are times in the lives of those of us who seek to improve ourselves inwardly, and achieve worthwhile goals outwardly, that we may wonder if it is possible to do both. Throughout history, we have seen those who have done so, and we long to emulate them. In the many biographical profiles I've read it has been noticeable that every one of them has encountered the same problems you and I face, and many persons haven't done as well with those problems as we do. So let's put that attractive illusion aside for a few moments. Let us examine a few core principles on our diverse paths to self-growth and achievement that will help us progress toward a better life.

To begin, we must distinguish between the "phenomena" others have demonstrated and the goal of your life. Everyone doesn't win an Academy Award or the Masters Golf Tournament. There isn't enough room on the stage or even the golf links for that. So how do we rearrange our thinking without giving up the goal of a better life?

There are twin goals for each of us: growth, and achievement. Growth is an inner phenomenon. Achievement is an outer phenomenon. If both the inner and outer are improved during

your lifetime, have you been a failure? Only if you stop growing and achieving, so long as you are physically and mentally
able to continue. If you improve your inner and your outer life
(most especially your relationships with others) you are a success. Strange as it seems, there are three basic elements from
the ancient wisdom that allude to this modern process of self-
growth and achievement.

The first is the exercise of self-control. Think of it simply
as self-discipline. The finest performers and achievers in every
human activity control and discipline themselves in a hundred,
possibly a thousand, different ways. Food, speech, relationships,
studies, money management (spending/saving) are but a few
examples. You can think of more that are pertinent to your life
and circumstances. Don't attempt to deal with all of them at
once. A very few at a time will do nicely.

The second element is the ability to focus and concentrate.
You've probably experienced becoming so absorbed in
something you are reading, watching on television, or perhaps
simply thinking about, that you never even hear someone call
your name, nor are you interrupted by outer distractions. You
have "lost track of time," is your explanation. I would say that
you have been concentrating. So you already possess the ability to concentrate, but you may need to practice focusing it
with deliberate intent to develop the ability to a greater degree.

One way to practice concentration is to select an object upon
which you center your attention as you deliberately ignore
or at least reduce your awareness of interruptions by both

internal and external stimuli. Resist allowing your attention to waver from the object of your concentration. Choose simple objects for this practice. Examples are an apple, candle, book cover, flower, a picture or statue. As I write this I pause to concentrate on the inexpensive pen I'm using. For the first time, after writing thousands of words using the same brand, I notice there is a tiny figure of a man drawing a line around the brand name of the pen. Study each of the various items you use for practicing concentration until you become practiced at noting details that previously escaped your attention.

The third element for promoting self-growth and achievement is to develop the ability to harmonize with the energies of the animate and the inanimate. In other words, with the energies of all living things, including the human kingdom, and kingdoms of the lower animal, vegetable, and even the mineral.

This study cannot include ways in which to accomplish the innumerable harmonizing techniques except to suggest the use of the mantra Om and the full Om Mani Padme Aum. I offer you this technique to aid the harmonizing process:

Place a living plant at heart level on a table. Face it at a distance of three or four feet. Center your concentrated attention upon it as you chant Om or the full mantra from three to six times. Then pause, but maintain your concentration. If it wavers, return to it.

Do you feel in either your heart or your solar plexus that you are part of the living organism you are facing?

Do you sense the perhaps small but real energy it radiates? Do you detect "something" flowing from you to the plant? Is it encouragement? Appreciation? Love? Or some other quality?

What prompting comes to you as a result of what you feel or sense? Do you wish to touch the plant lightly? Speak to it? Move it to a place where it receives better sunlight? Whatever promptings you receive are an experience in harmonizing your self with the energies of another living form of life.

After you have become somewhat practiced at this experiment, attempt the same process, but in place of the plant think of someone you know, but who is not present with you. Similar feelings and questions may be used. But remember, this is a process of harmonizing, of creating "oneness." It is not a process of manipulating the life of either plant or person. It is a method of harmonizing, of encouraging, of sharing and loving. It is a means of stimulating self-growth and achievement with the help of the mystic mantra.

Oᴍ

— the Breath

— the Sound

— the Mind

Oм — the Breath — the Sound — the Mind

The rishis and gurus of a time too ancient to date, gave their entire lives to creating and refining the mantra. It is not difficult to imagine a solitary seeker of the spirit, researching the "scientific" relationship between the divine and the human, spending long days chanting the embodiment of spiritual thoughts into sounds. Probably centuries were required for the various experimenters to compare, refine and agree upon the exact words of the mantra. Thereafter it resisted change, no matter the language, because it was the simplest and purest way of expressing the originators' purpose — to blend the oneness of the spiritual with the diversity of the material.

One of the great secrets of mystical practice is the connection between breath, mind and speech. Scriptural references of many kinds refer to it. "In the beginning...Oм"..."the breath of God moved"..."God said, let there be light." There is always a combination of breath, speech, and thought.

A mystical puzzle must have entered the minds of the ancients on innumerable occasions. "What is the mysterious relation between breath, speech and mind? Why is it that Oм sounded without thought of breath does not produce the same vibrational result as OM with specific breath? Why does the word OM spoken casually not have the same effect as OM chanted? What causes sound to be produced to accompany breath?"

Some of these questions the ancients could not answer for they did not possess the knowledge of anatomy available to us today. And some we cannot answer even today because they are of a higher level of reality. But let's experiment a few moments, as those of long ago must have done, so that you personally can go through a similar process of discovery.

First, simply breathe normally a few moments. Make no sound. Nothing happens. You are not aware of any inner vibrational change. It's the same body processes you've engaged in throughout your lifetime. Repeat several breaths simply to become aware of the feeling. Then inhale a few deeper breaths to note the slight physical change, usually a slight increase of energy.

Next speak the word OM normally as you would any word you use frequently. Some minor responses — both in body and mind — may be observed at this point in your experiment, however they are probably minimal.

Finally, after a deeper than normal inhalation, chant OM during a full exhalation. Note how the sound seems to reverberate through your head and throat areas, and to a lesser degree throughout your entire body. Depending upon the acoustics of the room, you may also become aware of the sound reverberating throughout the space in which you are conducting this experiment.

Coupled with this experiment, our knowledge of anatomy helps reveal more information about the process. Unlike any other organ, your vocal cords are fastened only at the sides. This allows them to vibrate, like the reeds of an organ, creating sound. Your vocal cords do not vibrate unless you think them into doing so! They do not vibrate normally unless you are exhaling! And this is how breath, body and mind function together!

Breath without mind creates no sound.

Breath modified by mind creates sound, changes pitch, volume, forms words.

Breath, mind and sound combined create sound of a specific vibrational nature which induces specific responses of a similar nature, both within your being and in the outer world around you.

Chanting is merely sustaining the sound of spoken syllables. Instead of OM as a short, clipped word, it's "oh" (sustained through slightly parted lips during half the exhalation) then "mmm" (sustained through closed lips for the second half of the exhalation).

To give greater resonance and vibrational power to the chant, be sure to expand your abdomen as you inhale, and contract it as you exhale.

When chanting OM MANI PADME AUM, sound the entire mantra during exhalation.

Either OM by itself, or the entire mantra, chanted by a group of any number of like-minded people, produces a vibrational harmony that is wonderful to experience. The cohesion of energy, the unity from diversity thus obtained, is a spiritual dynamic that lifts the consciousness of the entire group. Oneness with each other, and with something greater than each other, is frequently the result.

One English version of Oₘ Mani Padme Aum is "I am the jewel in the lotus." For many persons, this rendering becomes so meaningful that it is often used as a concentration or affirmation phrase when dealing with a variety of situations.

For a moment think of some of the inferences that may be drawn from this spiritual, symbolic statement. For example, saying "I am the jewel in the lotus," may really mean "I am a spark of the eternal flame, the eternally glistening jewel in the lotus of the physical body." Or, "I am the life essence of the Divine."

Other inferences could include, "I am the flame which is ignited as spiritual energies are infused into earthly energies." "I am the spark which calls my Self, my talents, my resources, into the path of action." "May the light be my daily companion."

"May the inner light guide me to the greater light." "May I continue to develop my talents, my understanding, my insights into wisdom, both human and divine."

Where and how should I use the English language rendering of the mantra?

• as the core seed thought for a period of simple relaxation.

• as an inspirational seed thought for (strengthening) arousing physical energy, for calming emotional energy, for clarifying mental energy.

• as the central seed thought of a meditative time for attuning to your own inner, higher Self.

• as an uplifting spiritual idea for raising your consciousness level to a higher degree.

• as an inner method for temporarily freeing yourself from the pressure of material level problems such as work stress, relationship disharmonies, illnesses, and so on.

Swami Parampanthi says some ancient gurus speak about Bija (seed) mantra. In other words, each mantra has an inner seed (*Bija* in Sanskrit), or essence. They say that the chanter needs to enter into the seed of a given mantra and *realize* and manifest its full potency and meaning. The revelation manifests itself as the seeker chants the mantra with devotion and concentration by penetrating the sound to discover the inner revelation.

The seed thus becomes a full-grown tree!

Thus, he who can enter the seed of the mantra can speed up its germination into a tree and can enjoy its fruits, as it were.

Parampanthi says, "By chanting the mantra with devotion and regularity, the chanter enters into the mantra or vice-versa. The chanter and the mantra become one and all the transforming potency of mantra becomes the possession of the chanter. He thus absorbs the power of the mantra. Thus, by chanting OM MANI PADME OM the chanter becomes the Jewel, the enlightened Being, the Luminous One like the radiant Jewel.

"In the larger sense it is a process of *osmosis*. A chanter by chanting day and night "God! God!" becomes God as it were

by absorbing all godly qualities and virtues, as his psyche, consciousness, unconscious, etc. are flooded only with the vision
and thought of God — the meditator becomes the object of his
meditation. This is a very ancient belief."

Healing
with the
Mantra

Healing with the Mantra

Alternative healing methods are finally finding popular favor as legitimate therapeutic techniques. In some instances, an alternative form of treatment is used by itself. In other situations one or more of the alternatives are used in combination, and often even merged with conventional allopathic medicine and surgery. I propose that mystic mantras may very well play a part in any healing process, by themselves or in combination with other therapeutic methodologies.

How can a chant help heal? By inducing a physical response to the vibrational sound of the chant. Does this seem unlikely, even impossible?

There are many mantras other than the one we're discussing here which begin with the word OM that are specially beneficial for healing. To give you a list would be a disservice, for they vary greatly in their fitness for each individual. They should be prescribed by an expert in Sanskrit who can match individual mantras with the physical and psychological profiles of the person who wishes to use them.

Thomas Ashley-Farrand, a friend and colleague, is such a person. At my request he gave me a mantra that I wished to use in support of conventional medical treatment, as well as the kind of spiritual treatment I was already using. An immediate response amazed me and possibly you'll find it interesting too.

The problem for which I wished to use the mantra is common to men, an enlargement of the prostate gland. During a leisurely moment after receiving the mantra from Thomas, I became quiet and relaxed...then I chanted the mantra. My mind was not centered upon anything except trying to speak the unfamiliar Sanskrit words which were a little difficult for me. After the third attempt, it was as though an entity other than myself jolted my mind and forced my attention to the problem area. At the same moment I knew that no outer agency was involved. It was the vibrational result of speaking the mantra, even with absolutely no mental attention to the problem on my part. I immediately understood the reason for the ancient definition of OM as a "thunderbolt," a forceful phenomenon arising from the spoken word.

In the days that followed, speaking the mantra brought on a similar but gentler result. Higher energies certainly continued their work, clearing the inner atmosphere of its conflicting activity. I continue to use the mantra.

A trained vocalist can shatter a drinking glass by the sustained sounding of a note that resonates with the glass. Even inanimate matter responds to sound, but being rigid and brittle, the glass shatters. Not so with the human body. It also responds to sound, particularly its own sound as various parts of the body resonate with the human voice.

To aid in healing your body, or any part thereof, chant either OM, or the full mantra from as many as one to a dozen times daily, in one session or divided into several. Specific body areas that are particularly sensitive to chanting include the chakras or energy centers, brain, heart, solar plexus, gonads, bloodstream, nerve systems and all muscles.

Your body also possesses its own form of consciousness, and will direct your attention during your chanting to the area where the spiritual resonances will serve best. Always chant with the intent to lovingly massage, calm or stimulate the area involved. Try to feel the flow of vibrational influence as your OM or other chant is sounded.

Is it possible to use OM MANI PADME AUM as a component in the process of self-healing? I believe it is, but I must say it may be unwise for most persons to rely upon it alone. Perhaps its greatest benefit in this area is to serve as an aid to concentration and spiritual focus upon the desired result of any type of therapy.

Speaking the mantra changes the vibrational structure of every atom in your physical body. The connection between the nature of your mind as you speak the mantra and the resulting structure of the atoms in your body is remarkable. They are vibrational reflections of each other. Here are some suggestions for using the mantra in connection with self-healing.

First, be at ease as you would for any meditation process. Maintain this state of physical, emotional and mental relaxation until you feel you are in touch with something or someone greater than yourself. Remember, release physical tensions, creating a minimum of tautness of physical muscles. Release emotional and mental tension. Release cares and worries of physical plane life. Your body should feel weightless, as though you could, if you wished, simply float away. In this state of complete physical ease, speak the mantra slowly:

OM — MA-NI — PAD-ME — AUM

Let the sound of the mantra sink deeply into the depths of your consciousness as you hear it with both outer and inner ear. Remember there are vibrational levels within you, and residents in higher levels around you, both bringing energies of strength and vitality to you. Now speak it again:

OM — MA-NI — PAD-ME — AUM

A radiant light (perhaps invisible) is created by your words and thoughts. Sense that you are absorbing the sounds and the light into your entire being, just as a sponge slowly absorbs a liquid. For a time, savor this feeling as the sound and light flood every part of your body, your emotional nature, your mind and spirit. Savor the power. Not one part of your self remains untouched, unchanged. There is cleansing. There is purifying. There is healing. Speak it once more:

OM — MA-NI — PAD-ME — AUM

Now feel the harmony. Feel the harmony that is being expressed by every part of your self — from the lowest to the highest — nothing but clean, pure harmony. Every segment of your being is in harmony with every other segment. Feel the increase of strength, vitality, wholeness, light. And feel the in-flow of divinity, of the Divine Presence.

Bring this mantric self-healing procedure to a close with the following benediction, or your personal version of it:

> Almighty Architect of the Universe, I, child of Thine who seeks the Light, come now further into it, and receive it, for strength, vitality, peace and health on every level of my life. I express to the Supreme One my joy at receiving this divine in-flow, and will use it in building a greater life. Peace. OM MANI PADME AUM. OM SHANTI.

If you wish to use the mantra to direct healing energy to others, follow your personal adaptation of this same method. Instead of mentally directing the energies to flow inward to yourself, direct them outward to the person to whom you wish to send the healing.

Be
Peaceful
with
OM SHANTI

Be Peaceful with
Om Shanti

At the conclusion of spoken or written passages the words Om Shanti (pronounce it shahn´- tee) are often used.

Shanti means peace. Quiet, restful, silent peace. Combined with Om it means peace so calm it seems that breath itself nearly ceases. It is bathed in universal silence. It is the motionless lotus floating on the boundless pool of life.

In the calmest possible state of body, emotions, mind and spirit, repeat it several times, mentally or orally: Om Shanti — Om Shanti — Om Shanti. As you do so, allow a "vibrational holy oil" to flow throughout your self, calming, healing your being on every level of your self, your life.

Om is the sacred universal sound. Shanti directs that sound toward universal peace, and toward personal peace.

Each powerful sound in the two word phrase serves as vibrational support for the other. As in a well constructed building, each piece of lumber and masonry, even each nut and bolt, contribute to the strength of the entire house, so do these two simple words empower each other.

Peace on a cosmic level is wonderful, but peace in you and your life is another matter. Intoning the mantra isn't by itself a magical formula for dispersing turbulence in your life circumstances. Though Jesus calmed the waves while standing in a small boat on the stormy Sea of Galilee, his connection with the elements was more developed than yours and mine. What he did was a symbolic example of what we can accomplish in our personal lives. We can calm disturbing situations in life to a degree, but we must not rely on the power of the mantra alone. We must support its action in the invisible by our active presence in the visible. The chant does not do it all. What must *you* do?

Answers to this question can be supplied only by your circumstances, your needs and aspirations, the talents you already possess and the new ones you are developing. Carefully examine all these aspects to determine the actions *you* will take to help create peaceful situations.

Remember that the mantra OM SHANTI creates reverberations on all life levels. When using the mantra, ask this question: "Where in space do I desire to create vibrational elements that may contribute to peace and harmony? In my family? In myself? My community? My place of employment? The world? On the level of physical matter? Or the emotional? The mental? Or the spiritual?" By specifically designating *where*, you reinforce the mantra's energies and their effects. Be careful, however, when thinking of *what* you would like to accomplish or the steps needed to produce a specific result. Neither you nor I are wise enough to attempt altering another person's life pattern, their karma or dharma, to suit our personal desires.

And I hope neither of us is foolish enough to attempt doing so. Speaking the mantra to connect the shanti center in another to the shanti center in yourself, is wise — to manipulate the center in another, or attempt to do so to satisfy your own wishes, is not a privilege either of us possesses.

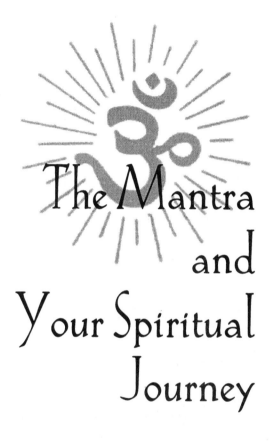

The Mantra
and
Your Spiritual
Journey

The Mantra and
Your Spiritual Journey

OM MANI PADME AUM is a spoken symbol of the universe. It verbally portrays the universe in its entirety, collectively, and in its individual aspects.

The mantra refers to the heavens, the Upper World, the energies of a higher vibrational nature — the energies of Light. They may be the energies of human consciousness, or of the human body. Or they may represent energies of the Divine Spirit. It matters not for they are all Light.

There are times when an understanding of a matter is deepened by an investigation of its parts and how they function as a whole. An interesting intellectual exercise that may lead to a measure of spiritual realization is to probe inner meanings of the mantra by dividing it into its six syllables. The syllables are: OM — MA-NI — PAD-ME — AUM.

Mythical teachings from the ancient past light our way to a revelation of the word OM as the first syllable of the entire mantra. In that respect it is an allusion to the ancient gods and the "state of godhood" which exists, slumbering, in each human being. There, it awaits inner resurrection to the highest and purest possible expression of spirituality — the Infinite flowing unimpeded through the finite. The symbolic color of the syllable OM is white.

The second syllable — MA of the word MANI — refers to those who are more than mortal yet less than gods. We might think of them as those who have attained the highest degree of Mastership, titans of spiritual understanding beyond our own comprehension. The color representing this attainment is purple.

The third syllable — NI of the word MANI — symbolizes those who have become adepts. They are high upon the path of attainment. Not yet Masters, they are close to attaining that high degree. They have become proficient at incorporating spiritual life and energy into all facets of life on earth. The color associated with this state of attainment is blue.

The fourth syllable — PAD in the word PADME — suggests those who are disciples, seekers on the spiritual path, those who not only study spiritual principles but also practice them to the best of their ability. This comprises the majority of students and practitioners of the metaphysical, deeper spiritual, mystical and esoteric in the world today. These persons are active in their outward serving as well as their inward seeking — and the color which portrays them is a color of activity, yellow.

The fifth syllable — ME of the word PADME — signifies another human aspect — the human being who is at the beginning of the upward journey. This is the yearner who is ready to become the seeker. This is the person who stands upon the shore of the unknown and is inwardly prompted to discover what lies beyond physical perception. This is one who is suddenly aware of a growing spiritual consciousness, is dissatisfied with the superficial and will not rest until the great journey of realization is begun. The color associated with this syllable is green.

Note that the first five syllables of the mantra suggest an order of spiritual accomplishment that is unlike the conventional creeds of any religion. They lead to the final mantric syllable of AUM, sometimes spelled HUM, which is symbolically associated with all the vital principles which make possible the exciting and fulfilling journey from ignorance to enlightenment.

AUM is a glorious "Amen" of joy as it activates all the vital principles which make the spiritual journey possible. It coalesces and focuses the life energies as one undertakes the journey through the awakening spiritual consciousness, discipleship, adeptship, mastership and the ultimate "state of godhood." It gathers into one stream the light-filled energies of all planes and makes them available for the human being to control and use. The color is indigo.

AUM or HUM — the pronunciation is essentially the same — is the syllable that restarts the journey to the heights, spiral after spiral, until it need no longer to be revisited. Thus the review of the mystic mantra, syllable by syllable, is a constant reminder of the nature and purpose of life through all levels and all ages.

Finding Everyday Magic in Spiritual Mantras

Finding Everyday Magic in Spiritual Mantras

Using the term *magic* in connection with OM MANI PADME AUM can easily lead to misunderstanding. It is not intended to refer to stage legerdemain or unfounded superstition. Unfortunately there are those who view it in that sense. They simply have not as yet glimpsed the Great Light nor taken any steps toward it. The idea of magic is here used in the sense of a human relationship with energies that have as yet been only partially discovered by scientific inquiry.

Continuing scientific discoveries will improve the influential relationship between human beings and forces of a higher vibratory nature, activated through prayer, affirmation, mantra, meditation and ceremony. All these methods have been the subject of research, mantra probably to a lesser degree than the others. However the mantric combination of sound, in the form of the human voice, mind or attitude, symbolism and the significance of certain words gives mantras a high place among the methods by which the human accesses the more than human.

It is often difficult to find a spiritual antidote for the turbulent world that surrounds us. The energies of life tumble and

swirl around us in chaotic fashion as we cope with our responsibilities. It seems that our sense of spiritual peace succumbs
to the force of earthly gravity. On an intellectual level we understand this isn't true, but what key is available to free ourselves to yearned-for oneness with factors greater than our
physical selves? There are many, of course, and all of them are
good and proper. I suggest your chanting OM MANI PADME AUM,
OM by itself, or OM SHANTI, even if only briefly, on a daily
basis, as a definite key.

The best time to do this is as near as possible to the beginning of your day. The reason for this is because the mantra is
traditionally an invocation. In any spiritual meeting place, or
ceremony, the invocation is for the purpose of gathering spiritual energies and making a functional connection with them.
It is the starting point for the initiations of the day.

The mantra invokes (brings in, or up, or activates) principles and energies that are attuned to more peaceful vibratory
fields as well as those that are more definitely related to your
unique life purposes.

A variation of placing a written version of the mantra in a
prayer wheel is to carry it on your person as a talisman. First
let us discriminate between the idea of a talismanic mantra and
a rabbit's foot, or other "lucky" piece. To look upon it as the
latter is mistakenly and superstitiously placing power in a pow-
erless object. A stray piece of wood, or a button off my shirt,
would do as well. The mantra, considered in this manner, does
not itself bring you good fortune. As a spiritual talisman,

however, it frequently helps you focus your attention upon
factors which benefit you in one way or another.

The words of the mantra may be written on slips of paper
or cards, engraved upon bits of leather, metal or other materi-
als, and carried on your person. The result is that doing so brings
the words, and the meanings you associate with them, more
often and more actively into your consciousness. It is the power
of your mind and spirit, complementary energies through the
mantra, and the thoughtful attention you give to the entire process, that has a beneficial effect upon the energies of your life.
If you use it as a talisman, do so with careful attention to your
attitude and method. Do not allow the practice to degrade into
using it as a charm or lucky piece.

OM MANI PADME AUM may be used as a method for impreg-
nating a material object with one or more spiritual energies.
This is specially true of articles intended for spiritual use. The
mantra may stand by itself, or be combined with any prayers
and meditative practices with which the user has his or her own
affinities. A partial list of material objects most suitable for
this purpose would include a cross, rosary, holy water, crystal,
stone, gong, candle, perhaps a treasured heirloom.

A suggested method of using the mantra for this purpose
would be to begin by placing the object on a stand or table, or
hold it in your hands, as you enter a calm, meditative state.
Attempt to feel a strong sense of rapport between your inner
self and the object. When you feel this has been accomplished,
continue to hold the object at the center of your awareness as

you slowly (either mentally or, most preferably, aloud) chant the mantra. As you do this, have in your mind the idea that spiritual energies are flowing through you into the article. Continue this process as long as you feel comfortable with it, or until your intuitional sense suggests the process is completed. You may wish to repeat the process at another time until you feel satisfied that the method has fulfilled its desired purpose.

It has been said that frequent use of the mantra removes obstacles from the pathway of a person who is seeking spiritual progress. It is believed that vibrational energies activated for this purpose have a cleansing effect on the inner vision of a seeker.

This result from speaking the mantra is specially appreciated by persons who use it in conjunction with practicing various forms of yoga, particularly hatha yoga. Speaking the mantra while motionless in each position of the yogic "Salutation to the Sun," for example, equally spaces the intervals of the position and at the same time adds higher vibrational energies to the strictly muscular activity.

Chanting the mantra listlessly or tentatively is considerably less effective than doing so with a firm and positive voice. There are times, however, when it may be inappropriate to voice the chant aloud. In a public place, a busy shopping mall for example, you may wish for the benefit of a few moments' inner atmosphere of peace and spirituality. A restaurant chair, corridor bench, or even a quiet corner in a store, will allow you to relax as you mentally chant OM MANI PADME AUM or OM SHANTI. Actually this is an excellent exercise in self-control and concentration. Practicing it from time to time will improve your ability to remain calm in disturbing circumstances and inharmonious relationships.

There are those who believe that repeating OM MANI PADME AUM a thousand times enables one to gain whatever is wished for. To me this seems quite unrealistic. Rapid repetition of the mantra causes one to concentrate on words only and thus lose continued awareness of their meaning and their spiritual connection. Speaking the mantra slowly, while maintaining awareness of your heartfelt connection with your purpose in doing so is, in my opinion, a much more effective way to gain its many benefits. The intent of your heart is far more precious than the dexterity of your tongue.

Does speaking the mantra create an aura of personal protection? Does it create a magic circle of defense against all harm, a ring-pass-not, a spiritual sanctuary against every manner of material calamity? Not if it contradicts karma. Nor does it replace common sense in the conduct of your life.

On the other hand, there is no question but that it does create a vibrational aura in which one's awareness of surrounding circumstances is heightened. In this sense it does protect against physical harm or injury, against disease, against numerous unfavorable situations and events. Depending only upon the mantra as a protective device might well be compared to driving a car without brakes. It is not a method for shifting your personal responsibilities in life to another. It is not a "karma dodger."

Meditate with the Mantra for Personal Unfoldment

Meditate with the Mantra for Personal Unfoldment

Remember the ancient Hermetic principles that energy follows thought, activity results from attention, the nature of the activity corresponds with the nature of the thought.

For stimulating the progress of your personal spiritual growth, whatever you are thinking as you meditate and speak the mantra becomes a *cause* which results in a specific *effect*, as do all causes. Subtle changes in your self, your life, and your life circumstances arise from the combination of spoken mantra and silent meditation. Each, the sound and the silence, has its own energy levels and functions. Each in its own way transmutes the energies of your life to their own higher purposes. Unbelievable as the process may seem, the divine and the human become truly one in their movement toward realization of the spiritual purpose you have selected. The higher octaves of that purpose may not always be visible to your physical level perception. Believe in them. They will come.

Jacob's ladder is the Biblical symbol of this process. He "saw" angels ascending and descending upon the ladder, and the heavens were opened. In other words, the mingling of divine and human energies resulted in activities on levels not normally accessed by the normal human consciousness. Jacob's higher consciousness was aroused, and greater than normal perceptions were activated.

Meditation is important to personal progress. It need not be engaged in exactly as described in this book. You must certainly make allowances for your personal affinities in the process. There are many ways to meditate. Use your intuition regarding which are best for you. In most all of them, an essential ingredient is centering your attention inwardly upon the higher spiritual level centers — the chakras. In doing so, your aura, or energy field, begins expressing its harmonious relationship to the divine purposes of your higher mind, or soul. The divine in you becomes more harmonious with the Divine that is everywhere.

Among many people of the Orient, it is said that OM MANI PADME AUM is the chariot upon which the human being rides to the gates of heaven and the door of Divinity. In other philosophies it would be thought of as the chariot of the gods — gods being personifications of higher than human energies.

In a slight and semantic variation of using OM MANI PADME AUM in personal everyday life, consider fine tuning your thought processes from meditation to aspiration — the latter oriented more to the achievement of outer than of inner goals. All our destinations are not spiritual and eternal. Incarnated as we are in physical substance, on occasion it is the material and temporal that needs our attention — our earthly aspirations.

In general, follow the same methodology for aspiration as for meditation. In the latter, attention and energy direction are inward. For the attainment of material goals and other successful ventures in life (that is, for realizing aspirations) attention and energy direction are mentally guided outward and into the goals themselves.

For the improvement of intuitional and other forms of psychic sensitivity, such as clairvoyance and clairaudience, speak the mantra in moments of tranquil meditation. At the same time center your attention upon the chakras, one by one from lower to higher. This concentration of vibrational energy activated by your thought, and the vibrational sound of the mantra, stimulates the chakras. They in turn are brought into the special type of harmonious relationship which is receptive to psychic communications.

Using
a Gong
with the
Mantra

Using a Gong with the Mantra

Scientists tell us that the Earth creates a sound as it speeds through space. The Earth's tone, though inaudible to our ears, may be likened to the sustained sound of a bell or gong that continues to reverberate long after it has been struck. Is it too farfetched to suggest that perhaps the Earth itself is chanting OM? Hindu belief is that the vibrational sound of OM created the Earth. Thinking of this idea brings to my mind the picture of elongated iron filings, spread randomly on a flat surface, suddenly assuming a definite organized pattern when a magnet is passed over or under them. Did the magnetic energy pattern of the cosmic OM organize the randomly chaotic energies of life into the vast systems of the universe? Some think of OM as the *sound of the soul of the universe.*

If you accept the idea that there may be correlations between these concepts and your personal life, you may wish to experiment with striking a gong or bell — then as the tone continues to reverberate chant OM — MANI — PADME — AUM. As the sound of the gong slowly fades away, meditate quietly. Then repeat the process for as many as four or five times if you wish. Do not overdo it. Most people will find that a larger number of repetitions begins to dilute the effectiveness of the process.

Using a gong with the mantra is an excellent method of creating a special inner atmosphere of spiritual reflection. It is not necessarily for producing any other result. What the mantra and gong together do depends upon the intent and spirit of the one who uses this spiritual practice.

The
Mantra
and
Visualization

The Mantra and Visualization

As a frequent and general method of using OM MANI PADME AUM for connecting yourself with greater and higher energies, you may wish to couple it with the practice of visualization.

For example, the mantra's meaning, "I am the jewel in the lotus," may be visualized in your mind's eye. Mentally see yourself centered in an iridescent aura as you speak the mantra and feel energy flowing *into* your being.

If you wish to project energy to another person or outer circumstance, visualize "I am the candle (or light) in the lotus." Mentally see yourself as a candle, or light, as you speak the mantra and feel energy flowing through and *away from* you into the person or circumstance you have designated.

The principle is: illumine the jewel; radiate the light. Energy flowing *in*. Energy flowing *out*.

In
Closing

In Closing

This book explores the mystic mantra as an aid to spiritual discovery and a course of spiritual action. You as reader and I as author have together examined numerous ways to use the mantra in fulfillment of these purposes.

OM MANI PADME AUM — while speaking it, either mentally or aloud, serves to delete, layer after layer, distractions of all kinds which scream for our attention. Physical urges, commercial interests, political clamor and a thousand other voices join in an attempt to urge us down the material path that totally excludes the spiritual.

Using the mantra regularly, or even occasionally, serves to aid the process of integrating the higher with the lower, the spiritual into its proper "mix" with the material. It accomplishes this objective by focusing attention, objectively as well as subliminally, upon the mystical descent of spirit into matter.

Then, in the course of daily events, the objective memories and the subliminal messages of the spiritual rise to a certain level of expression in the consciousness. The result is: the divine becomes human and the human becomes divine. "I am in the Father and the Father is in me," is the Christian Era statement of this process. From the pre-Christian Era to today it is said that "OM signifies the Infinite, and AUM signifies the Infinite in the finite."

OM SHANTI

OM MANI PADME AUM

The publisher of this book is a nonprofit organization presenting metaphysical, mystical, philosophical and self-help material. For more information on books by the author write:

Astara Administration Building
P.O. Box 5003
Upland, CA 91785

E-MAIL: **mail@astara.org**

WEBSITE: **www.astara.org**